CRAZY
for
COFFEE

Crazy for Coffee
©2018

www.AmazingMediaWorks.com

ISBN-13: 978-1-947676-24-4

CONTENTS

HOT COFFEE DRINKS

Black Forest Coffee

8 oz French Roast Coffee
4 tbsp chocolate syrup
2 tbsp Maraschino cherry juice

1/4 c whipped cream
1 tbsp chocolate chips
2 cherries

Combine coffee, chocolate syrup, & cherry juice. Pour into 2 six oz cups. Top with whipped cream, chocolate chips, and cherry.

Café Au Lait

2 c hot French Roast coffee
2 cups hot milk

Pour from separate warm pots or pitchers into warm coffee cups simultaneously.

Cafe De Olla

2 c water
1/4 c coarsely ground Mexican Coffee
2 cinnamon sticks
1 tbsp brown sugar

Combine water, coffee and brown sugar in saucepan, heat to boiling. Reduce heat, simmer 3-5 minutes, and strain. Serve in warm mugs, and place cinnamon stick into mug.

Tropical Mocha

1 oz coconut syrup
1/2 oz cherry syrup
1 oz chocolate topping
1 shot espresso
steamed milk

Combine espresso with toppings into 8 oz cup. Fill with steamed milk, and top with foam.

Spice Coffee

8 tbsp coffee grounds
8 c water
Peel of one large orange
Peel of one large lemon
30 cloves
4 tsp sugar

Place coffee and spices in coffeemaker's basket Add water and brew.

Mexican Coffee

2 tbsp chocolate syrup
1/2 cup whipped cream
1/4 tsp cinnamon
1/2 tbsp brown sugar
2 cups espresso roast coffee

1. Whip together chocolate syrup, whipped cream, cinnamon, sugar and nutmeg.
2. Add hot coffee, mix well, and pour into 4 warm coffee mugs.
3. Top with whipped cream, and lightly dust with cinnamon.

Normandy Coffee

Espresso roast coffee
2 c apple juice
2 tbsp brown sugar
3 orange slices
2 cinnamon sticks
1/4 tsp allspice
1/4 tsp cloves

1. Combine ingredients into 2 qt sauce pan. Bring to boil, reduce heat and simmer for 10 minutes.
2. Strain mixture into warm coffee pot. Pour into cappuccino cups, garnish with cinnamon stick.

Jamaican Black Coffee

6 cups espresso or French roast coffee
1 thin sliced lemon
2 thin sliced oranges
1/3 cup sugar
3 tbsp rum

1. Place lemons, oranges, and coffee in 2 qt saucepan. Heat to just before boiling, and add rum and sugar.
2. Stir until sugar is dissolved, and remove from heat.
3. Ladle into warm coffee cups, and garnish with lemon slices.

Cafezinho

8 tbsp Costa Rican coffee (finely ground)
2 c cold water
1 tsp sugar

1. Put water into 1 qt saucepan and bring to boil.
2. Place coffee into strainer lined with cheesecloth (or Cafezinho bag).
3. Pour boiling water over coffee into coffee pot or hot pitcher.
4. Add sugar to taste.

Georgia Coffee

3 c Espresso roast or
French Roast coffee
1/2 c whipped cream
1 can (16 oz) peaches

1 1/2 tbsp brown sugar
1/4 tsp cinnamon
1/8 tsp ginger

1. Drain peaches, and set aside syrup.
2. Combine 1/2 the coffee and peaches in blender, and mix on medium setting for 1 minute.
3. Combine 1 c cold water, sugar, cinnamon, ginger, and peach syrup in 2 qt saucepan.
4. Bring to boil, reduce heat, simmer for 1 minute.
5. Add coffee and peach mixture, stir well, and ladle into 8 oz warm coffee cups.
6. Top with whipped cream and serve.

Turkish Coffee

1 1/2 c cold water
4 tsp French Roast or Italian Roast coffee (grind as fine as possible)
4 tsp sugar

1. Heat water in 1 qt saucepan to lukewarm. Add coffee and sugar, bring to boil, stirring occasionally.
2. Pour 1/2 coffee mixture into espresso cups, and bring remaining coffee back to boil. Spoon off foam into cups, fill cups, but do not stir.

Christmas Coffee

1 c medium roast coffee
1 tbsp brown sugar
1 egg yolk
1/2 c cream nut meg

1. Combine sugar and egg yolk, beat until smooth.
2. Heat cream in small saucepan, and slowly mix in eggs and sugar. Heat to just before boiling.
3. Pour coffee into 2 warm cups and top with egg and cream mixture. Gently dust with nutmeg.

Orange Coffee

1 c strong coffee
1 c hot chocolate
2 orange slices
Whip cream
Dash of cinnamon

1. Mix coffee and hot chocolate.
2. Place one orange slice into each cup.
3. Pour coffee mixture into cups.
4. Top with whipped cream, and garnish with cinnamon.

Macadamia Fudge Cappuccino

2 shots Espresso

1 oz chocolate fudge syrup

1 oz macadamia nut syrup

steamed milk, (whipped)

sweetened cocoa power

In a 12 oz cup, combine syrups and espresso. Fill with steamed milk, top with whipped cream, and lightly dust with cocoa powder.

Raspberry Torte Breve

1 shot Espresso

1 oz raspberry syrup

1/2 oz crème de cacao syrup

steamed milk

In a 12 oz cup, combine syrups and espresso. Fill with steamed milk.

Cafe Borgia

2 cups strong Italian coffee

2 cups hot chocolate

whip cream

grated orange peel (garnish)

Mix coffee and hot chocolate, Pour into mugs. Top with whipped cream and orange peel.

Java Grog

Grog Mix:

2 tbsp butter (softened)
1 c brown sugar
1/4 tsp ground cloves
1/4 tsp nutmeg
1/4 tsp cinnamon

Mix all ingredients until smooth and creamy. Divide grog mix into 6 warm 8 oz coffee mix. Add hot coffee to fill each mug, stir well.

Toffee Coffee

1/4 c sugar
3/4 c hot water
1 1/2 c hot chocolate
2 c medium roast coffee

1. Melt sugar in a hot skillet. Stir constantly until sugar is golden brown and melted.
2. Remove from heat, slowly add hot water until caramel is dissolved. Add hot chocolate and coffee.
3. Place back on heat and simmer to blend. Pour into warm coffee mugs.
4. Top with whipped cream if desired.

After Dinner Mint

1/2 lb whole bean coffee

2 tbsp mint flavoring

1/2 c unsweetened cocoa

1. Blend coffee and mint in small mixing bowl.
2. Place on baking sheet, bake at 200 °F for 1 hour.
3. Grind coffee for Espresso machine.
4. Mix ground coffee and cocoa powder.
5. Brew coffee according to directions of coffee brewer.
6. Store leftover coffee in air tight container in freezer.

Spice Coffee

8 tbsp coffee grounds

8 c water

Peel of one large orange

Peel of one large lemon

30 cloves

4 teaspoons sugar

Place coffee and spices in coffeemaker's basket. Add water and brew.

Caribbean

1 coconut

2 c milk

4 c strong coffee

1 tbsp sugar

1. Punch two holes in to coconut, pour liquid into saucepan.
2. Bake coconut for 30 minutes at 300 °F.
3. Break open coconut, remove meat, and grate.
4. Mix coconut meat, coconut liquid, and milk in a sauce pan. Heat over low heat until creamy. Strain.
5. Toast grated coconut under broiler.
6. Mix milk mixture, coffee, and sugar.
7. Pour into mugs, garnish with toasted coconut.

European

1 c strong coffee

1 egg white

1/4 tsp vanilla extract

2 tbsp half and half

1. Beat egg white until forms soft peaks.
2. Gently add vanilla, and continue to beat to stiff peaks are formed.
3. Place into 2 coffee mugs.
4. Pour coffee over egg white.
5. top with half and half.

Grog

3 c coffee
1/2 c heavy cream
1 c brown sugar
2 tbsp softened butter
1/4 tsp ground cloves
1/4 tsp ground nutmeg
1/4 tsp cinnamon

1. Peel of one large orange, broken into 6 pieces.
2. Peel of one large lemon, broken into 6 pieces.
3. Place one piece of each peel into cups.
4. Mix butter, sugar, cloves, nutmeg and cinnamon
   Mix coffee and cream.
5. Pour both mixtures into cups and stir.

Irish Coffee

2 c strong coffee
2 tbsp orange juice
2 tsp lemon juice
whipped cream

1. Mix coffee, orange juice and lemon juice.
2. Pour into Irish whiskey glass.
3. Top with whipped cream.

Mediterranean

8 c strong coffee
1/3 c sugar
1/4 c chocolate syrup
1/2 tsp aniseed (tied in cheesecloth)
20 cloves
4 cinnamon sticks
whip cream
orange and lemon twists

1. Place coffee, sugar, chocolate syrup, aniseed, cloves and cinnamon into a sauce pan.
2. Heat to 200 °F over medium heat.
3. Strain into mugs.
4. Top with whipped cream and twists.

Cafe con Miel

2 c hot coffee
1/2 c milk
4 tbsp honey
1/8 tsp cinnamon

Heat everything until warm, but not boiling.
Stir well to dissolve honey, and serve.

Cafe Speciale

4 tsp chocolate syrup

1/4 tsp nutmeg

1/4 c heavy cream

1 tbsp sugar

3/4 tsp cinnamon

1 1/2 c extra-strength hot coffee

1. Put 1 teaspoon chocolate syrup into each of 4 small cups.
2. Combine cream, 1/4 teaspoon cinnamon, nutmeg and sugar.
3. Whip until well blended
4. Stir remaining 1/2 teaspoon cinnamon into hot coffee.
5. Pour coffee into cups. Stir to blend with syrup.
6. Top with whipped cream.

Café Alpine

8 oz fresh brewed medium roast coffee

2 tbsp brown sugar

1 tsp vanilla extract

1 tsp water

1. Split coffee and vanilla between 2 mugs.
2. Dissolve the sugar in 1 tsp water, and heat in a saucepan to boiling.
3. Mix in the larger portion of hot water, then pour into the two mugs.
4. Stir well and serve.

Mexican

2 c water
1/4 c coffee grounds (ground coarsely)
1 tbsp brown sugar
1 cinnamon stick

1. Place all ingredients into a sauce pan.
2. Bring to a boil, reduce heat and simmer for 5 minutes Strain into mugs.

Mexican Mocha

1 1/2 c strong coffee
4 tsp chocolate syrup
3/4 tsp cinnamon
1/4 tsp nutmeg
1 tbsp sugar
1/2 c whipping cream

1. Put 1 teaspoon of chocolate syrup into each cup.
2. Mix whipping cream, 1/4 teaspoon of the cinnamon, nutmeg, and sugar.
3. Whip until you have soft peaks.
4. Place the last 1/2 teaspoon of cinnamon into coffee, and stir.
5. Pour coffee into cups, stir to mix in chocolate syrup.
6. Top with whipped cream mixture.

Mocha

2 c coffee

1/3 c cocoa

2 c milk

1/2 tsp vanilla extract

1/2 c whipping cream

1/8 tsp cinnamon

1. Mix cocoa, sugar, coffee and milk in a sauce pan.
2. Heat, over medium heat constantly stirring, until simmering.
3. Remove from heat and stir in vanilla.
4. Pour into cups, top with whipped cream and cinnamon.

Viennese

1/2 c chocolate

2 1/2 c strong coffee

4 tbsp light cream

2/3 c heavy cream

1 tsp sugar

Dash of cinnamon

Dash of cocoa

1. Melt chocolate in sauce pan.
2. Stir in light cream.
3. Slowly add coffee, beating until frothy.
4. In a cold bowl whip heavy cream and sugar.
5. Pour coffee mixture into cups.
6. Top off with heavy cream.
7. Garnish with sprinkle of cinnamon and cocoa.

Nogged Coffee

1 c coffee
1 egg yolk
1/2 c cream
dash of nutmeg

1. Beat sugar and egg yolk together.
2. Place cream into sauce pan, and heat over low setting.
3. Whisk in egg mixture.
4. Heat to 200 °F.
5. Pour coffee into to cups, and top with cream mixture garnish with nutmeg.

Cafe Caribe

4 tbsp ground coffee (fine)
1/2 tsp grated orange peel, dried
1/4 tsp cinnamon
1-inch piece of vanilla bean
1/8 tsp ground cloves

Blend ingredients well. Brew by your usual method.

ICY COOL DRINKS

Iced Coffee Milkshake

1 pt milk
2 oz brewed coffee
3 tbsp sugar
6 ice cubes

Mix ingredients into blender. Blend until thick and creamy.

Granita Al Caffe

4 oz Espresso ground coffee
8 oz sugar
2 pt cold water
1 egg white

1. Place water and sugar in 2 qt saucepan. Heat to boiling, and boil until sugar is completely dissolved.
2. Remove from heat, add coffee to sugar mixture, and let sit for 10-15 minutes. Strain liquid, let cool.
3. When cold, pour syrup into covered ice tray, and place in freezer until partially frozen (30-40 min.) Beat egg white until stiff.
4. Place sugar mixture into bowl, mix in egg white, and return mixture to ice tray.
5. Freeze until firm, and smooth, beating every 30-40 minutes to break up ice crystals.
6. Serve in dessert dish topped with whipped cream.

Amaretto Cooler

1 c brewed Amaretto flavored coffee
1 c milk
1/2 tsp vanilla
1/3 tsp almond extract
1 tbsp sugar
1/8 tsp cinnamon

1. Mix coffee, milk, vanilla, almond, and sugar into pitcher.
2. Stir until well mixed.
3. Pour over ice into 2 twelve-ounce glasses.

Coffee Smoothie

1 c skim milk
2 tbsp sugar (or equivalent of sugar substitute)
2 tbsp chocolate syrup (regular or lite)
1 tbsp instant coffee granules
7-10 ice cubes

Blend for two to three minutes on high speed of blender.

Banana Blender

1 ripe banana
1 1/2 c cold medium roast coffee
3 tbsp sugar
3 large scoops vanilla ice cream

1. Cut banana into small pieces, and mix with coffee and sugar in blender.
2. Blend at high speed until smooth and creamy.
3. Add ice cream, and blend on medium speed until mixture is creamy.
4. Pour into 12 oz glasses and serve immediately.

Koffe Frappe

2 c cold French roast coffee
1/4 tsp vanilla
1 1/2 c crushed ice
6 tbsp sweetened condensed milk
Whip cream

1. Mix milk, coffee, vanilla, sugar and ice in blender.
2. Blend on medium high speed until smooth and creamy.
3. Pour into tall glasses and top with whipped cream.

Caribbean Chiller

3 c lukewarm medium roast coffee

8 lemon slices (sliced thin)

8 orange slices (sliced thin)

1 pineapple slice

1. Place fruit slices in large mixing bowl.
2. Add coffee, and stir to mix up fruit juices and coffee.
3. Place in freezer and chill for 1 hour.
4. Remove from freezer, stir again, then remove fruit.
5. Serve over ice in tall glass.

Espresso Cooler

1 shot espresso

1 scoop French vanilla ice cream

1 c cold milk

1 oz French vanilla syrup

Whip cream

1. Mix espresso, milk, syrup, and ice cream in blender.
2. Blend on medium speed for 2 minutes.
3. Pour into tall milkshake glass.
4. Top with whipped cream and chocolate shavings.

Continental Cooler

1 1/2 c cold French roast coffee

1/2 tsp Angostura Bitters

1/2 tsp vanilla

1 1/2 tbsp sugar

1 c club soda

4 orange slices

1. Mix coffee, bitters, vanilla and sugar in blender.
2. Blend on low speed 2 minutes.
3. Serve over ice in 10 oz glass, 2 inches from top.
4. Top off each glass with club soda and orange slice.

Tropicana Coffee

4 c cold strong coffee (French or espresso roast)

1 c milk

1 tsp rum flavoring

1 tbsp sugar

1 c club soda

1. Mix milk, rum flavoring, and sugar in pitcher.
2. Stir until sugar is dissolved.
3. Place in refrigerator and chill for 1 hour.
4. Pour 1 cup chilled mixture over ice in tall glass.
5. Add coffee, leaving 2 inches of room.
6. Top off with club soda.

Icy Mocha Mint

3/4 c cold med roast coffee   2 tbsp chocolate syrup
1/4 c milk   2 drops mint extract

1. Mix coffee, chocolate syrup, mint and milk in blender.
2. Fill blender with ice, and blend on med. High speed until foamy. Serve in tall glass.

Mocha Frosty

2 1/2 c cold strong coffee (French roast or espresso roast)
5 tbsp chocolate syrup
1 pt coffee ice cream

Mix all ingredients in blender. Blend on medium high until smooth. Serve in tall Sunday glasses.

Cafe Mazagran

1/2 c cold strong coffee (Mexican or Costa Rican recommended) 1 tsp sugar
1/2 c club soda
Mix coffee and syrup.

Pour over crushed ice, and add club soda.

Coffee Float

2 1/2 c strong coffee
2 teaspoons sugar
2/3 c cream
4 scoops of coffee flavored ice cream
1 large bottle of cola (such as Coke)

1. Sweeten coffee with sugar, and chill.
2. Mix coffee and cream.
3. Fill 4 glasses half full.
4. Add 1 scoop ice cream to each glass.
5. Top each glass with your favorite cola.

Cafe Au Vin

1 c cold strong French roast coffee
2 tbsp granulated sugar
dash cinnamon
2 oz Tawny port
1/2 tsp grated orange peel

Combine ingredients and mix in a blender cup at high speed. Pour into chilled wine glasses.

Homemade Coffee Smoothie Recipe:

1 c of coffee chilled
1 tsp of sugar, honey, or chocolate syrup (to flavor to
your liking)
1 banana cut into chunks
1/2 c of whole milk

Blend the milk, coffee and bananas until there is a
smooth texture. Taste to see if it is to your liking, add
the sugar or honey and blend until desired flavor.

Cafe Frappe Recipe

1 egg white
1/2 c cold water
1/2 c ground coffee
4 c boiling water
1 c sugar

1. Beat egg white slightly.
2. Add cold water and mix with coffee.
3. Add mixture from above to boiling water. Continue
    to boil one minute.
4. Let cool for ten minutes. Strain. Add sugar.
5. Freeze to a mush. Serve in frappe glasses with
    whipped cream, sweetened and flavored.

Cinnamon Caramel Iced Coffee

6 tbsp ground coffee
1/2 tsp cinnamon
1/2 c caramel dessert syrup

1. Mix the cinnamon and the ground coffee and brew a pot of coffee as usual.
2. Add the syrup to the hot coffee and stir until dissolved. Chill through and serve over ice, with milk or sugar to taste.

Thai Iced Coffee

2 c of water
1 tbsp of sugar or maple syrup
Ice cubes
1/4 c of half-and-half or evaporated milk
3 cardamom pods (this adds the unique Thai flavor)
1/3 c whole gourmet coffee beans, dark roast or 1/4 cup ground dark roast gourmet coffee

1. Grind the cardamom pods with coffee beans. Now brew this mixture with 2 cups of water. Add sugar or maple syrup and let it cool.
2. Pour this into two glasses filled to the top with ice. Add half-and-half or evaporated milk.

Ginger Fruit Mocha

1 shot espresso

1 oz chocolate syrup

1 oz peach syrup*

1 oz ginger syrup

8 oz cold milk

* use your favorite fruit (pear, apple, banana, apricot etc.).

Coffee Frosty

1/2 cup cold dark roast brewed coffee

1/2 cup dry milk

1/4 c sugar

1/2 c crushed ice

1-pint coffee flavored ice cream

1. Mix dry milk with 1/2 cup cold water in bowl.
2. Mix with beater 4-5 minutes until peaks form (like meringue).
3. Add sugar and coffee while mixing on low speed.
4. Add ice cream slowly.
5. Pour into four 10-12-ounce glasses.

Coffee Banana Smoothie

3/4 to 1 c fresh brewed coffee, cooled
1 medium banana, peeled
1 to 2 tbsp sugar or honey, to taste (optional)
1 1/2 c French vanilla yogurt (low-fat or nonfat is fine)
1 to 2 tbsp protein powder or other nutritional powder
(optional)
1 tsp chocolate syrup (optional)
Vanilla extract (to taste)

1. Twenty to thirty minutes before you plan to mix
   your smoothie, put the coffee in a shallow pan and
   place it in the freezer, stirring once or twice after 15
   minutes until slushy.
2. Thinly slice the banana onto a plate and put that in
   the freezer as well, to chill.
3. While you're waiting, chill 2 or 3 glasses for serving.
4. When you're ready to proceed, combine the chilled
   coffee, banana, and sugar to taste in a blender.
5. Blend just until smooth.
6. Add the yogurt and any of the remaining
   ingredients you desire to use.
7. Blend again, briefly, just until smooth.

Maple Walnut Mocha

1 shot espresso

2 oz maple nut syrup*

1 oz chocolate syrup

8 oz cold milk

* Also try pecan, macadamia, or hazelnut

Banana Frosty

1 1/2 c cold dark roast brewed coffee

1 banana

3 tbsp sugar

1 c French vanilla ice cream

1. Cut banana into chunks.
2. Mix all ingredients in blender 1 minute on high speed.
3. Add ice cream, blend 1 minute on medium speed.
4. Pour into two 12 oz glasses.

Mocha Mist

2 1/2 cups cold medium roast brewed coffee

1-pint coffee ice cream

2 oz chocolate syrup

Combine ingredients in blender. Blend on high 2-4 minutes. Serve in four 12 oz glasses.

Toffee Coffee

1/2 c cold dark roast brewed coffee
2 c French vanilla ice cream
1 toffee candy bar (such as Heath)

1. Place coffee and ice cream into blender. Mix on low speed 1 minute.
2. Break candy bar into small pieces, add to blender.
3. Blend on high 1-2 minutes (until candy bar is well blended).
4. Serve in two 12 oz dessert glasses.

COFFEE:

(n.) survival juice

LUSH LATTES

Tropical Iced Latte

1 shot espresso
2 oz banana syrup
1 oz passion fruit syrup*
8 oz cold milk

1. Mix syrups and espresso in blender.
2. Add milk, and 2 cups crushed ice.
3. Blend on high setting 1 minute.

You may like to substitute for coconut, mango, or pineapple syrup.

Mandarin Chocolate Latte

1 shot Espresso
1 oz chocolate syrup
1 oz mandarindo syrup
steamed milk
orange-flavored whipped cream

1. In 8 oz cup, combine syrups and espresso.
2. Fill with steamed milk, and top with whipped cream.
3. Sprinkle with chocolate sprinkles.

Cactus Latte

1 shot espresso
2 oz raspberry syrup
1 oz kiwi syrup

1 oz lime syrup
8 oz cold milk

Cabo Mocha Latte

1 shot espresso
1 oz chocolate syrup
1 oz orange syrup

1 oz coconut syrup
8 oz cold milk

Mai Tai Latte

1 shot espresso
1 oz rum flavored syrup
1 oz orange syrup

1 tsp grenadine
1 tsp lime juice
8 oz cold milk

Raspberry Guava Latte

1 shot espresso
2 oz raspberry
1 oz guava syrup
8 oz cold milk

Melba Latte

1 shot espresso
2 oz peach syrup
1 oz raspberry syrup
8 oz cold milk

Eggnog Latte

2 c eggnog
1 tbsp rum
1 tbsp bourbon
1 c hot coffee

1. Heat eggnog until hot (do not boil).
2. Blend with liqueurs and coffee in a blender until nog is frothy. Serve warm.

Grande Caffe Latte

2 (1 1/4-ounce) shots espresso, hot
12 oz milk, steamed to 150 °F

1. Pour both espresso shots into the bottom of a cup.
2. Add steamed milk until cup is 3/4 full, holding back the foam.
3. Top off the drink with velvet foam from steamed milk.

Baklava Latte

1 oz praline syrup
1/2 oz maple walnut syrup
1 tsp lemon syrup
1/2 oz hazelnut syrup
1 shot espresso
steamed milk
cinnamon
1 cinnamon stick.

1. Combine syrups and espresso in warm 10 oz cup.
2. Fill with steamed milk, top with foam.
3. Sprinkle with cinnamon, and garnish with cinnamon stick.

Mint Mocha Latte

2 oz whole milk
2 tbsp chocolate syrup
1 tsp mint extract
2 c freshly brewed espresso (chilled)
2 c crushed ice
2 mint leaves

1. Combine ingredients in blender with crushed ice
   Blend on high speed 2-3 minutes.
2. Garnish with mint leaves.

Elegantissimo

2 c freshly brewed espresso
1/2 c sugar
1 oz semi-sweet chocolate, finely chopped
1/4 c heavy cream
2 c crushed ice

1. Combine hot espresso, sugar and chocolate Stir until sugar dissolves, and chocolate melts Refrigerate 3-4 hours, until well chilled.
2. Pour into blender with crushed ice. Blend on high 3-4 minutes. Pour into tall glasses.
3. Whisk cream until soft peaks form Spoon onto glasses.
4. Garnish with shaved chocolate.

Caramel Nut Latte

1/2 oz caramel syrup
3/4 oz chocolate syrup
1/2 oz hazelnut syrup
1 shot espresso steamed milk

Combine syrups and espresso in 8 oz cup. Fill with steamed milk.

*may also be topped with whipped cream and nuts

Blanco Cappuccino

1/2 c whole milk
1 tsp vanilla extract
1 tsp brown sugar
6 oz freshly brewed espresso roast coffee
Ground cinnamon

1. Combine milk and vanilla in saucepan Heat to boiling.
2. Add sugar, return to heat to dissolve sugar.
3. Place milk in blender, blend on high 3 minutes.
4. Add espresso and 2 cups crushed ice. Blend on high 2-3 minutes.
5. Serve in short glasses.
6. Dust with cinnamon.

I Only Need Coffee on Days Ending with "y"

ALCOHOLIC COFFEE DRINKS

Café Brulot

3 c Espresso roast (original recipe calls for Chicory)
24 sugar cubes
4 c cloves
Rind of 1 orange (grated)
Rind of 1 lemon (grated)
2 cinnamon sticks
3/4 c Cognac or Brandy

1. In 2 qt saucepan, combine all ingredients except coffee.
2. When hot, ignite and flame Brandy.
3. When fire extinguishes, slowly pour coffee stirring to mix while pouring.
4. Ladle into warm cups.

Frosty Brandy

1 c strong black coffee (Sumatran suggested)
2 oz Brandy   1 c half and half
2 tbsp sugar   4 ice cubes
1/4 c whipped cream

1. Mix sugar, ice cubes, and coffee in blender, and blend on medium for 25-30 seconds.
2. Add half and half, and brandy, blend for additional 10-15 seconds.
3. Top with whipped cream (optional).

Bandito Coffee

8 c French roast or espresso roast coffee

8 oz Tia Maria or Kahlua

4 oz Tequila

1/2 pt whipping cream

1 oz unsweetened cooking chocolate

2 tsp sugar

1 tbsp orange juice

1. Whip cream until thick enough to peak, mix in sugar and orange juice, and refrigerate.
2. For each cup, place 1 oz each of tequila, and coffee liquor in coffee cup, fill with coffee, and top with whipped cream. Dust with shaved chocolate.

Jamaican Kicker

2 c strong black coffee (French or Espresso roast)

2 oz Kahlua or 2 oz Tia Maria

2 oz Dark Rum

1/4 c whipped cream

1. Mix Kahlua or Tia Marie and rum in 2 cups of coffee (1 oz each).
2. Add hot coffee, top with whipped cream, sprinkle with nutmeg.

Hot Mint Julep

2 c strong black coffee

5 oz Bourbon

2 tbsp sugar

2 tbsp heavy cream

2 sprigs mint leaf

1. Lace Bourbon and sugar into 2 large warm coffee mugs.
2. Add hot coffee and stir to dissolve.
3. Top with cream, but do not stir. Accent with mint leaf.

Grasshopper

1 1/2 c strong black coffee

2 oz crème de menthe

2 oz coffee liquor (Tia Maria or Kahlua)

1/4 c whipped cream

Dark and white chocolate after dinner mints

1. Pour 1 oz each of liquors into 2 tall latte glasses.
2. Fill with coffee and top with whipped cream.
3. Decorate with shavings of dark and light after dinner mints.

Hot Toddy

1 1/4 c very strong coffee (Espresso or French roast)
4 oz Calvados
2 oz peach or apricot Brandy
2-4 tsp sugar
1 1/2 tbsp heavy whipping cream

1. Place Calvados and brandy in small saucepan, and heat slowly, using low setting.
2. Add coffee, then sugar to taste.
3. While coffee is spinning from stirring, add cream but do not stir.

Pina Coffeelada

2 c strong cold coffee
2 oz tequila or 2 oz rum
1/2 oz coconut flavoring
1/2 tsp vanilla
2 c crushed ice
4 tbsp whipped cream
1/4 c Malibu

1. Combine all ingredients in blender.
2. Blend on high until smooth and creamy.
3. Pour into Pina Colada glass or tall drinking glass.
4. Top with whipped cream.

Velvet Hammer

1 oz vodka
1 oz crème de cacao
2 oz espresso
4 oz half and half
1 cup crushed ice

1. Combine vodka, crème de cacao, espresso & half and half into blender.
2. Blend on high 20 seconds.
3. Add crushed ice, blend another 20 seconds.
4. Immediately pour into 12 oz glass.

Café Vermouth

4 oz red vermouth
1 shot espresso
4 cups cold water
8 oz cold milk
2 oz crushed ice

1. In shaker or blender, combine vermouth, espresso, water, and milk.
2. Shake vigorously or blend on high 30 seconds.
3. Serve in tall cocktail glass.

Coffee Liquor

1 c water
2 c white sugar
2 c brewed dark roast coffee (cold)
1 tsp pure vanilla extract
1 1/2 c vodka

1. Boil water and sugar until dissolved
2. Turn off heat.
3. Slowly add dry instant coffee and continue stirring.
4. Add vanilla extract to the vodka, then combine the cooled sugar syrup and coffee solution with the vodka.
5. Cover tightly and shake vigorously each day for 3 weeks.
6. For Tia Maria, substitute brandy for vodka.

Calypso Coffee

1 1/2 oz Tia Maria
Hot Coffee
Whip Cream

Pour coffee into a coffee mug or Irish coffee mug, add Tia Maria and top with whip cream.

Irish

2 c strong coffee
2 tbsp orange juice
2 tsp lemon juice
whip cream

1. Mix coffee, orange juice and lemon juice.
2. Pour into Irish whiskey glass.
3. Top with whipped cream.

French Royale

1 oz Chambord
1 shot espresso
1 oz canned sweetened milk
1 c crushed ice

1. Combine Chambord, espresso and milk in blender.
2. Add crushed ice, blend on high for 30 seconds.
3. Serve in tall cocktail glass.

" You can do it."
- Coffee

Coffee Liqueur

4 c sugar
2 c water
2/3 c brewed coffee
10 coffee beans (whole)
fifth of Vodka*
1 Vanilla bean (2-3 inches)

1. Combine water, sugar, and coffee in a saucepan and bring to a full boil.
2. Skim off the froth and allow to cool thoroughly.
3. Pour into the container.
4. Add vodka, coffee beans (optional but will add a fuller flavor), and vanilla bean.
5. Store in a dark place for 3 weeks.
6. Strain and filter. Ready to serve.
7. *A brandy/vodka mix may be substituted for a simulated "Kahlua".

Note:
You can also use a rum/vodka mix to simulate "Tia Maria."
Yield: 1 1/2 quarts (may be halved)

Café Vienna

1 oz Kahlua
1 oz Crème de Cocao
2 shots espresso
4 oz hot chocolate
Whipped cream

1. Pour Kahlua and crème de cacao into a 10 oz coffee cup.
2. Add espresso and hot chocolate.
3. Top with whipped cream.

Café Bavaria

1/2 oz peppermint schnapps
1 oz Kalua
2 shots espresso
2 oz hot water

1. Mix peppermint schnapps and Kahlua into 10 oz coffee cup.
2. Add espresso and hot water.
3. Top with whip cream.
4. Garnish with peppermint stick.

Caribbean Java

1 oz dark rum
1 oz Tia Maria
2 shots espresso
4 oz hot water
Whipped cream

1. Pour rum and Tia Maria into 10 oz coffee mug.
2. Add espresso and hot water.
3. Top with whipped cream.

Cozy Coffee Amaretto

1 oz amaretto
2 shots espresso
4 oz hot water
2 tbsp coffee flavored ice cream
Nutmeg

1. Pour amaretto in to 8-12 oz coffee mug.
2. Add espresso and hot water.
3. Top with softened ice cream.
4. Lightly dust with nutmeg.

Caribbean Cruise

1 oz dark rum
1 oz amaretto
2 shots espresso
3 oz hot water
Whipped cream
Maraschino cherries with stems

1. Combine rum and amaretto into 10-12 oz coffee mug.
2. Add espresso and hot water.
3. Top with whipped cream.
4. Garnish with maraschino cherries or coffee beans.

Cabo Breeze

1 oz Kahlua
1 oz dark rum
2 shots espresso
2 oz heavy whipping cream

1. Combine Kahlua, rum, espresso, and whipping cream in blender.
2. Blend on high 30-40 seconds.
3. Serve over ice in 12 oz glass.

Café Pari'

1 oz brandy
1 oz Grand Marnier
2 oz espresso
2 oz hot water
Whipped cream

1. Combine brandy and Grand Marnier into 12 oz coffee cup.
2. Add espresso and hot water.
3. Top with whipped cream.
4. Garnish with orange slice.

Irish Warmer

1 oz Yukon Jack
1 oz Baileys Irish Cream
2 shots espresso
2 oz hot water
Whipped cream

1. Combine Yukon Jack and Baileys into 10 oz coffee cup.
2. Add espresso and hot water.
3. Top with whipped cream.

El Diablo

2 oz tequila gold
1 oz Kahlua
2 shots espresso
2 oz hot water
Whipped cream
Shaved chocolate

1. Combine tequila and Kahlua into 12 oz coffee mug.
2. Add espresso and hot water.
3. Top with whipped cream.
4. Sprinkle with shaved chocolate.

Espresso Nudge

1 oz brandy
1 oz crème de cacao
2 shots espresso
2 oz hot water
Whipped cream

1. Combine brandy and crème de cacao into 12 oz mug.
2. Add espresso and hot water.
3. Top with whipped cream.

Fruity Rum Heater

1 oz cherry brandy *

1 oz rum

1 tsp maraschino cherry juice

2 shots espresso

2 oz hot water

Whipped cream

1. Combine brandy and rum into 12 oz coffee mug.
2. Add espresso and hot water.
3. Top with whipped cream.
4. You may substitute cherry brandy for whatever flavor suits your taste.

*Optional replace cherry juice with flavor of brandy

Cabo Breeze

1 oz Kahlua

1 oz dark rum

2 shots espresso

2 oz heavy whipping cream

1. Combine Kahlua, rum, espresso, and whipping cream in blender.
2. Blend on high 30-40 seconds.
3. Serve over ice in 12 oz glass.

Louisiana Cooler

1 oz bourbon
1 oz praline flavor syrup
2 shots espresso
6 oz cold milk
1/2 cup crushed ice

1. Combine bourbon praline syrup, espresso and milk in blender.
2. Blend on low setting for 20-30 seconds.
3. Add ice to blender, blend on medium another 20 seconds Strain into 12 oz glass.

White Russian

1 oz Kahlua
1 oz vodka
4 oz cold espresso
4 oz half and half

1. Combine Kahlua, vodka, espresso, and cream in shaker or blender.
2. Shake vigorously or blend on medium high 30 seconds.
3. Serve over ice in 12 oz glass.

Café Cognac Cooler

8 oz brewed dark roast coffee, chilled

3 oz cognac

2 oz coffee liqueur

2 oz half and half

2 scoops coffee ice cream

1. Combine cognac, coffee, coffee liqueur, half and half in blender.
2. Blend on Medium high 30 seconds.
3. Serve in 12 oz glass.
4. Top with ice cream.

Café Vermouth

4 oz red vermouth

1 shot espresso

4 cups cold water

8 oz cold milk

2 oz crushed ice

1. In shaker or blender, combine vermouth, espresso, water, and milk.
2. Shake vigorously or blend on high 30 seconds.
3. Serve in tall cocktail glass.

☑ COFFEE

☑ COFFEE

☑ ANOTHER COFFEE

I LOVE CHECKING THINGS OFF
MY TO DO LIST.

DELECTABLE COFFEE DESSERTS

Tiramisu

1 c mascarpone
1/4 c powdered (confectioners) sugar
2/3 c cold strong brewed coffee (recommend Sumatran or Costa Rican)
1 1/4 c heavy cream
3 tbsp coffee liquor (Kalua or Tia Maria)
4 oz ladyfingers
2 oz semisweet chocolate chips
Unsweetened cocoa powder

1. Line a loaf pan with plastic wrap or waxed paper.
2. Mix mascarpone and powdered sugar in large mixing bowl, beat for 60-90 seconds.
3. Add 2 tbsp of coffee, mix thoroughly.
4. Add 1 tbsp liquor to cream and mix until cream is stiff and forms peaks, add 1 tbsp.
5. To mascarpone mixture, mix thoroughly, fold in rest of mixture.
6. Place 1/2 of mixture in Loaf pan, smooth and level top.
7. Put remaining coffee in bowl for dipping ladyfingers.
8. Dip ladyfingers on one side, and place on top of mascarpone in single layer.
9. Add remainder of mascarpone to loaf pan, smooth and lever top and repeat dipping.
10. Proceed with remaining ladyfingers.
11. Cover with plastic wrap, and chill 4-6 hours.

12. Turn tiramisu out of loaf pan by placing serving tray over pan and flipping.
13. Dust top lightly with cocoa powder.
14. To serve, cut into slices.

Kahlua Muffins

3/4 cup half and half   1/2 c chopped pecans

1/4 c Kahlua or Tia Maria   2 tbsp sugar

1 box chocolate fudge cake mix

1 1/2 cups melted butter

1 pkg cream cheese (8 ounce)

3 tbsp brewed dark roast coffee

1. Grease 24 muffin pans or line with muffin paper Preheat oven to 300 °F.
2. Measure 1 cup of cake mix and set aside.
3. Combine remaining cake mix, pecans and butter in mixing bowl.
4. Blend until entire mixture is moist and crumbly.
5. Press into bottom and sides of muffin tins.
6. Combine cream cheese, sugar, Kahlua or Tia Maria, and coffee, add in remainder of cake mix and egg, mix until smooth slowly mix in half and half, mixing well Divide mixture among muffin tins.
7. Bake 45-55 minutes.
8. Let cool, then place in refrigerator to allow crusts to set firm (2-4 hours).

Beignets

3/4 c whole milk
1/4 c brewed dark roast coffee

2 tbsp sugar	1 tbsp shortening
2 tsp dry yeast	1 tsp salt
3 c all-purpose flour	1 egg
1 tsp nutmeg	Confectioners sugar

1. Mix milk and coffee.
2. Heat to boiling point (do not boil).
3. Mix shortening and sugar till well blended.
4. Slowly add 1/2 flour mixture to milk, stirring to melt shortening and dissolve sugar.
5. Cool to room temperature. Add yeast, mix thoroughly.
6. In separate bowl, combine flour, nutmeg and salt Slowly add milk to form smooth batter.
7. Add eggs, blend well.
8. Add remaining flour, mix until smooth.
9. Cover with towel, allow to rise (approx. 1 hour).
10. When dough has risen to double size, knead and roll out to 1/4 inch thick. Cut into diamond shapes with knife or cookie cutter.
11. Place on cookie sheet, cover and allow to rise about 1-hour.
12. Heat light cooking oil to about 385 ºF. Fry the beignets to golden brown, turning only once Lay on paper towel to drain.
13. Dust liberally with confectioners sugar.

Espresso Chocolate Mousse

8 oz plain chocolate

3 tbsp brewed cooled espresso

2 tbsp butter

4 eggs, separated

8 oz plain chocolate

4 serving cups

For each cup:
1. Cut 12-inch square foil, fold in half, mold around bottom of drinking glass.
2. Repeat for 3 more cups.
3. Melt chocolate in small pan set over boiling water Spoon chocolate into foil cups.
4. As it cools, spread it up sides of foil with back of spoon Refrigerate until firm and set hard Mousse.
5. Melt chocolate as before, adding espresso to chocolate.
6. When melted and smoothly mixed, add butter slowly.
7. Remove from heat and stir in egg yolks.
8. Whisk egg whites until stiff, then fold into chocolate coffee mix.
9. Pour into bowl and refrigerate 3-4 hours.
10. Scoop chilled mousse into chocolate cups.
11. Top with whipped cream.

Tarratoga Torte

Base:

3 egg whites
1 c of castor sugar
1 tsp of baking powder
1 c of finely chopped pecans or walnuts
2-3 tsp of very finely ground coffee (pulverized)
14 Sao biscuits finely crushed

Topping & Filling:

1 1/2 c of thick (double) cream
1-2 tsp of castor sugar to taste
2-3 tbsp maple syrup (optional)
1 small block of dark chocolate

1. Beat the egg whites until stiff and gradually add the sugar and other ingredients.
2. Preheat oven to 375 °F. Grease 8-inch cake tin.
3. Spoon the mixture evenly into the tin and bake approximately 40 minutes.
4. Cool for 30-40 minutes.

Topping:
1. Beat the cream until stiff, adding the sugar gradually. If the mixture is not sweet enough for you add 3-4 teaspoons of maple syrup.

Decorate:
Place the base on a plate and cover with the cream mixture. Grate dark chocolate generously over the cream and chill for 2 hours before serving.

Coffee Toffee Pie

1 unbaked 9-inch chocolate graham cracker pie crust
3 eggs
1 1/2 c brown sugar
1/2 c freshly brewed dark roast coffee
2 tbsp melted butter
1 tsp vanilla
1 c semisweet chocolate morsels
1 1/2 c pecan halves

1   Preheat oven to 450 °F.
2   Mix eggs, sugar and coffee.
3   Blend with mixer on medium setting until smooth Blend in butter and vanilla.
4   Layer bottom of pie shell with chocolate chips and pecans.
5   Spoon mixture into pie shell. Bake for 5-7 minutes, reduce oven temperature to 325 °F, bake 25-30 minutes.

Layered Coffee Mousse

1 c strong black coffee (cold)
300g/10oz smooth creamed cottage cheese
1/2 c of vanilla sugar
1 c thickened cream, whipped
3 tbsp chocolate bits or grated chocolate
2 egg whites
8 - 10 Savoiardi (sponge finger) biscuits

1. Blend about one third of the coffee with the creamed cottage cheese and vanilla sugar.
2. Fold in whipped cream and about two thirds of the chocolate. Beat the egg whites until stiff and fold in the coffee cream cheese mixture to make a mousse.
3. Pour the remaining coffee into a deep plate and dip each biscuit briefly into the coffee.
4. Spoon about one quarter of the mousse into a glass serving bowl and cover with about half of the biscuits.
5. Add the remaining mousse and top with the rest of the biscuits.
6. Sprinkle the top with the remaining chocolate, and serve immediately.

Cafe Au Lait Pudding

1 package of Jell-O® brand vanilla instant pudding (2.5 oz.)
1 package of Jell-O® brand chocolate instant pudding (2.5 oz.)
3 1/2 c whole milk.
1 cup brewed medium roast coffee, chilled.
Whipped cream

1. Follow the directions on the package for preparing the vanilla pudding.
2. Add 2 cups of cold milk and pudding mix in a bowl and whisk for two minutes.
3. In a separate bowl, prepare the chocolate pudding.
4. The directions call for 2 cups of milk. Instead, put in 1 1/2 cups of milk, ½ cup of chilled coffee and pudding mix in a bowl. Whisk for two minutes.
5. Transfer about 4 tbsp of the vanilla and 4 tbsp of the chocolate pudding to a third bowl.
6. Add 2 more tbsp of coffee to this batch.
7. Whisk this batch. It should appear a few shades lighter than the chocolate pudding's color.
8. Discard the remainder of the coffee (or drink it).
9. Layer in cups or parfait glasses.
10. Refrigerate for five minutes.
11. Garnish with whipped cream before serving.

Espresso Cheesecake

1 1/2 c graham-cracker crumbs

2 tsp almond extract

6 tbsp butter or margarine (3/4 stick), softened

One 8-oz package semisweet-chocolate squares

Four 8-ounce packages cream cheese, softened

3 eggs

2/3 c sugar

1/3 c milk

2 tsp instant espresso-coffee powder

Lemon-Peel Twists (see below)

1 lemon (for garnish)

1. Prepare early in the day or a day ahead.
2. In a 9- by 3-inch spring form pan, use your fingers to mix graham-cracker crumbs, almond extract, and butter or margarine; press onto bottom and around the side of the pan to within 1 inch from top of pan and set aside.
3. Preheat oven to 350 °F.
4. In heavy small saucepan over low heat, melt 6 squares semisweet chocolate, stirring frequently.
5. In large bowl, with mixer at low speed, beat cream cheese just until smooth.
6. Add melted chocolate, eggs, sugar, milk, and coffee. Beat until blended.
7. Increase speed to medium; beat 3 minutes, occasionally scraping bowl with rubber spatula.

8. Pour cream-cheese mixture into crust in pan. Bake cheesecake 45 minutes. Cool in pan on wire rack.
9. Cover and refrigerate cheesecake at least 4 hours or until well-chilled. To serve, carefully remove cheesecake from pan. Coarsely grate remaining 2 squares semisweet chocolate.
10. Garnish top of cake with grated chocolate.

Coffee Chiffon Pie

1 uncooked 9-inch graham cracker pie crust
1 tbsp unflavored gelatin
4 eggs, separated
1/2 tsp salt
1 c sugar
1 tbsp lemon juice
1/2 c hot brewed dark roast coffee
3/4 cup cold brewed dark roast coffee

1. Soften gelatin in cold coffee (about 5 minutes).
2. Beat egg yolks, add 1/2 cup sugar, salt and hot coffee. Cook in double boiler until thick.
3. Add gelatin mixture and lemon juice. Allow to cool 5-10 minutes.
4. Beat egg whites with remaining sugar until stiff. Fold egg whites into coffee custard mixture. Place custard mix into pie pan.
5. Chill overnight, serve with whip cream.

Glazed Coffee Loaf

2 c all-purpose flour

3/4 c brown sugar

3 tsp baking powder

1 tsp salt

1 egg

1 c applesauce

2 tsp lemon juice

2 tbsp cooking oil

1 c walnuts

2 c semi-sweet chocolate morsels

1. Preheat oven to 350 °F.
2. Spray 9x5x3 loaf pan with non-stick cooking spray.
3. Blend flour, brown sugar, baking powder and salt in mixing bowl. Mix egg, applesauce and lemon juice together in small bowl, blend until smooth.
4. Add applesauce mixture and oil to flour mixture, stir just until blended.
5. Mix in chocolate chips and walnut. Pour into loaf pan, bake approx. 1 hour.

Coffee Glaze:

1 1/2 c confectioners sugar

2 tsp cool dark roast brewed coffee

3 tbsp brandy

1. Mix all ingredients and beat until smooth and creamy.
2. Allow loaf to cool for 10 minutes remove from pan and place on serving tray.
3. Dribble glaze over loaf while it is still warm.
4. Cool to room temperature, wrap, allow it to sit overnight before slicing.

Kealakekua Macadamia Cookies

1/2 c soft butter	1/4 tsp salt
1 c brown sugar	1/2 tsp nutmeg
1 egg	1/2 tsp cinnamon
1 3/4 c bakers flour	1 1/4 c raisins
1/2 tsp baking soda	
1 c chopped macadamia nuts	
1 c brewed chilled 100% Kona coffee	

1. Spray cookie sheet with non-stick cooking spray.
2. Combine butter, brown sugar and egg in mixing bowl.
3. Mix until smooth and creamy. Add coffee, mix well.
4. Stir in baking soda, salt, nutmeg, and cinnamon.
5. Slowly stir in flour, mix until smooth.
6. Add raisins and macadamia nuts.
7. Chill in refrigerator for 2 hours.
8. Preheat oven to 400 °F.
9. Drop by teaspoon on cookie sheet, 2 inches apart.
10. Bake 8-10 minutes until cookies are lightly browned.

Chocolate Coffee Truffles

12 oz plain chocolate
5 tbsp heavy whipping cream
2 tbsp Kahlua or Tia Maria
2 tbsp chilled dark roasted coffee
4 oz white chocolate
4 oz dark chocolate

1. Melt plain chocolate over double boiler.
2. Add whipping cream and liquor, mix until smooth. Chill mixture 4 hours, or until firm.
3. Divide mixture into 24 equal pieces, rolling each into little ball. Chill until firm again (approx. 1 hour).
4. Melt remaining plain, white, and dark chocolate into separate bowls.
5. Gently, using tongs, dip 8 each of the truffles into melted chocolates.
6. Place on wax paper, allow to set before serving.

NOTE: Due to use of fresh cream, truffles must be stored in refrigerator, and eaten within a few days*

- Good days start with coffee -

Coffee Crème Custards

2 1/2 cups whole milk   4 eggs
3 tbsp ground medium   4 egg yolks
roast coffee   3/4 cup sugar
1/4 cup sugar   4 tbsp water

1. Preheat oven to 325 °F.
2. Combine 3/4 cup sugar and water in small sauce pan.
3. Bring to boil stirring constantly, dissolving sugar.
4. Continue boiling until sugar is golden brown.
5. Quickly pour hot sugar mixture into 6 small oven proof dessert cups.

Custard:

1. Heat milk until almost boiling. Pour over coffee grounds, and let sit for 5-8 minutes.
2. Strain mixture into bowl to separate coffee grounds.
3. Mix in remaining sugar, eggs, and egg yolks.
4. Whip with whisk until mixed. Pour into dessert dishes.
5. Place dessert cups on cookie sheet. Add enough hot water to fill each cup 2/3 full.
6. Bake 30-35 minutes, until firm but soft. Cool 3-4 hours.
7. Gently run table knife around sides of custards and turn onto serving plates. Dust with brown sugar or chocolate shavings.

Petits Pots de Cappuccino

1 c medium roasted whole coffee beans
1 1/4 c whole milk
1 1/4 c whipping cream
1 whole egg
4 egg yolks

1. Preheat oven to 325 ºF.
2. Place coffee beans in sauce pan over low heat.
3. Heat for 3 minutes, shaking frequently.
4. Pour milk and cream over coffee bean.
5. Heat till almost boiling, stirring constantly.
6. Remove from heat, cover, and allow beans to soak about 30 minutes. Mix egg, egg yolks, sugar, and vanilla together.
7. Return milk to boiling, pour through strainer into egg mixture. Mix completely.
8. Pour mixture into 8 small baking cups and cover with foil.
9. Place in roasting pan, add water till 2/3 of cups are submerged.
10. Bake 30-35 minutes until firm but soft.
11. Cool to room temperature, then chill 2-4 hours.

Topping:

1/2 c whipping cream   3 tbsp ice water
2 tbsp sweetened chocolate powder

Mix whipping cream and water, whisk until thick, forming light peaks. Spoon onto custard. Dust with chocolate powder.

Coffee Zabaglione

4 cardamom pods   1/2 tsp vanilla extract
8 egg yolks   4 tbsp brown sugar
2 tbsp chilled brewed dark roast coffee
1/4 cup Kahlua or Tia Maria

1. Remove black seeds from cardamom pods and crush into fine powder.
2. Combine egg yolks, sugar, and cardamom seeds in mixing bowl. Beat until mixture is creamy.
3. Slowly add in coffee and liqueur. Place bowl over pan of boiling water.
4. Whisk until mixture is very thick and fluffy, and has doubled in volume. (Make sure water doesn't boil or mixture will curdle).
5. Remove from heat and divide into 4 dessert dishes. Dust with shaved chocolate, or crushed dark roasted coffee beans.

Sour Cherry Coffee Loaf

12 tbsp soft butter

1 c brown sugar

1 tsp vanilla extract

2 eggs lightly beaten

2 c all-purpose flour

¼ tsp baking powder

5 tbsp brewed dark roast coffee

1 c dried sour cherries

Icing:

1/2 c confectioners sugar

4 tsp brewed dark roast coffee

1. Preheat oven to 350 °F.
2. Lightly grease and flour large loaf pan.
3. Combine butter, sugar, and vanilla.
4. Mix until creamy.
5. Slowly add eggs, mixing well.
6. Add flour and baking powder.
7. Fold in coffee and 2/3 cup sour cherries.
8. Spoon into loaf pan and level top.
9. Bake about 1 hour, or until firm to touch.
10. Wait 5-10 minutes, and turn onto cooling rack.
11. Mix confectioners sugar and coffee for icing.
12. Mix in remaining cherries.
13. Spoon over top and sides of loaf.
14. Allow to set before serving.

Orange Coffee Scones

2 1/4 c all-purpose flour

1/2 tsp salt

2 tbsp sugar

1 orange rind, grated

4 tbsp butter

1/4 c brewed medium roast coffee

1/2 pint buttermilk

12 sugar cubes

2 c orange juice

1. Preheat oven to 475 °F.
2. Grease and flour cookie sheet.
3. Mix flour, salt, orange rind and sugar together, blend well. Fold in butter, mix until soft and crumbly.
4. Combine coffee and buttermilk, slowly add to flour mixture. Blend well to bind dough.
5. Roll dough out on floured surface to 1/2-inch-thick forming circle. Cut into pie slices and place on cookie sheet.
6. Dip sugar cubes in orange juice and press one into center of each scone.
7. Bake 10-15 minutes or until browned.

Coffee Date Cake

3/4 c butter   1/2 c sugar

1 c brown sugar   2 eggs

1/2 c whole pecans   1 c baking flour

1 1/2 tsp baking powder   1/2 tsp vanilla extract

1/3 c whole milk

1/2 c dates cut into small pieces

1/3 c brewed medium roast coffee

1. Preheat oven to 350 °F.
2. Combine 1/2 cup butter with brown sugar and coffee. Mix until smooth and creamy.
3. Pour mixture into 8x8 square cake pan.
4. Place dates and pecans in alternating circles around bottom of pan.
5. In separate bowl, cream together remainder of butter, sugar and eggs.
6. Add dry ingredients and vanilla, mix thoroughly.
7. Slowly add milk mixing until batter is smooth and consistent.
8. Pour batter over pecan and date glaze, leveling throughout pan.
9. Bake 40-45 minutes.
10. Immediately flip pan onto serving tray, but wait 5 minutes to remove pan.
11. Serve with whipped cream garnish with pecans.

Coffee Liqueur Cookies

2 eggs

2 1/2 c all-purpose flour

3/4 c packed brown sugar

1/2 tsp baking soda

1 c white sugar

1/4 tsp salt

1/3 c unsweetened cocoa powder

2 tsp instant coffee crystals

2 tbsp coffee flavored liqueur

1 cup butter or margarine, softened

2 c semisweet chocolate chips

1. Preheat oven to 300 °F (150 degrees C).
2. In a small bowl, dissolve instant coffee crystals into the coffee liqueur; set aside.
3. In a large bowl, cream together the butter, brown sugar, and white sugar. Gradually add eggs and coffee mixture while mixing.
4. Sift together the flour, cocoa, baking soda, and salt; stir into the creamed mixture. Stir in the chocolate chips.
5. Drop dough by rounded tablespoonfuls onto a cookie sheet.
6. Cookies should be at least 2 inches apart.
7. Bake for 23 to 25 minutes.
8. Immediately transfer cookies to cooling rack after baking.
9. These keep well at room temperature or refrigerated.

Chocolate Mousse Cake

4 eggs

1/2 c sugar

2/3 c all-purpose flour

1/4 c unsweetened cocoa

1/4 c Kahlua or Tia Maria Mousse:

2 tbsp dark roasted coffee beans (finely ground)

1 1/2 c heavy cream ½ cup sugar

1/2 c brewed dark roast coffee 4 egg yolks

1. Preheat oven to 350 ºF.
2. Grease and flour one 8-inch square, and one 9-inch round cake pan. Place eggs and sugar in pan.
3. Place pan over pan of boiling water, whisk until thick.
4. Remove from heat and whisk until stiff enough to leave trail by whisk.
5. Fold in flour and cocoa.
6. Pour 1/3 mixture into square pan, and remainder in round pan.
7. Bake square pan 15 minutes or until firm.
8. Bake round pan 30 minutes, or until firm.
9. After cooling, slice round cake in half horizontally.
10. Place bottom half back in pan, sprinkle with Kahlua or Tia Maria. Trim edges of square cake, use edges to line sides of pan. Place coffee for mousse in bowl.
11. Heat 1/4 cup of cream to almost boiling point, pour over coffee. Allow to set 5-6 minutes, then strain off coffee.

12. Place sugar in brewed coffee, heat until sugar dissolves. Heat to boiling, remove when heat reaches 225 °F.
13. Cool for 5 minutes, add egg yolks, whisk until very thick. Add remaining cream, whip until soft peaks form.
14. Spoon into cake shell, place in freezer for 20 minutes. Sprinkle remaining liquor over other cake.
15. Place on top of mousse, return to freezer for 4 hours. Dust with powdered sugar.

But First

COFFEE

SCRUMPTIOUS COFFEE CAKES

Chocolate Mousse Coffee Cake

6 oz plain chocolate

2 tbsp brewed French roast coffee

10 tbsp butter

1/4 c sugar

3 eggs

1/4 c ground almonds

Mascarpone coffee cream

1 c mascarpone

2 tbsp confectioners sugar

2 tbsp brewed French roast coffee

1. Preheat oven to 400 °F. Grease and flour 6-inch square cake pan. Mix chocolate and coffee in small pan.
2. Heat on low until chocolate is melted, stirring occasionally. Add butter and sugar, stir until dissolved.
3. Whisk eggs until small peaks are formed. Stir into chocolate and add almonds. Pour into cake pan.
4. Put cake pan into roasting pan, add water to cover 2/3 of cake pan.
5. Bake 45-50 minutes or until top is springy.
6. Cool 5 minutes, turn upside down to cool on serving tray.
7. Mix mascarpone with confectioners sugar and coffee Whip until smooth and creamy.
8. Dust generously over cake.

Cinnamon Coffee Cake

1 c sugar

2 tsp butter

1/2 tsp salt

2 c all-purpose flour

1 tsp baking powder

1/2 c whole milk

1/2 c brewed espresso 1 tsp vanilla

 4 tbsp melted butter

1 tbsp cinnamon

1/2 c sugar

1. Preheat oven to 325 °F.
2. Grease and flour 9x13x4 inch cake pan.
3. Blend together sugar, butter, and salt.
4. Mix baking powder in flour, and fold into sugar mixture slowly. Add milk and vanilla, mix well.
5. Pour into cake pan and bake 15-20 minutes.
6. In small bowl, mix cinnamon and remaining sugar.
7. Drizzle melted butter over cake, and sprinkle with sugar mixture. Bake 10 more minutes.

Coconut Coffee Cake

3 tbsp ground medium roast coffee

5 tbsp hot milk

2 tbsp sugar

2/3 c corn syrup

6 tbsp butter

1/2 c coconut flakes

1 1/2 c bakers flour

1/2 tsp baking soda

2 eggs

1 tsp Malibu coconut liquor

Frosting:

8 tbsp soft butter or margarine

2 c powdered (confectioners) sugar

½ c toasted coconut flakes

1. Preheat oven to 325 ºF.
2. Grease and flour bottom of 8-inch square cake pan.
3. Place coffee in small mixing bowl, and pour hot milk over coffee.
4. Cover and let stand 5 min.
5. Strain coffee, and set aside.
6. Mix sugar, corn syrup, and coconut.
7. Heat, stirring constantly, until butter and sugar are melted.
8. Add flour, baking soda, eggs, and 3 tbsp of coffee milk mixture.

9. Spoon into cake pan.
10. Bake 45 minutes.
11. Allow to cool in pan, then flip onto cooling rack.
12. While cooling, place softened butter into mixing bowl, and beat until smooth and creamy.
13. Fold in powdered sugar, and remainder of coffee.
14. Mix until smooth and creamy. Spread over top of cake, and decorate with toasted coconut.

Coffee Understands

Blueberry Coffee Cake

1 1/2 cups blueberries	6 tbsp butter
1 c sugar	1 egg
2 tbsp cornstarch	1/2 c buttermilk
1 1/2 c all-purpose flour	1/2 tsp vanilla
1/2 tsp baking powder	1/4 c vanilla
1/4 tsp baking soda	
1/4 c brewed medium roast coffee	

1. Preheat oven to 350 °F.
2. Combine blueberries with 1/4 cup water in sauce pan. Cook to boiling, reduce heat, simmer 5 minutes Stir in 1/4 cup sugar and cornstarch.
3. Cook until thickened, stirring constantly. Set aside.
4. Mix together 1/2 cup sugar, flour, baking powder and baking soda. Cut in 4 tbsp butter.
5. Mix till fine and crumbly.
6. Combine egg, coffee, buttermilk, and vanilla. Add to flour mixture, blend till just moist.
7. Spread 1/2 batter into 8x8x2 inch cake pan. Spread fruit mixture over batter.
8. Drop remaining batter by spoonful over fruit in random pattern.
9. Blend remaining sugar, flour, 2 tbsp butter fine crumbs Sprinkle over batter.
10. Bake 40-45 minutes or until golden brown.

Peach Coffee Cake

1/2 c butter, softened	1 tsp ground cinnamon
1/2 c granulated sugar	1/2 tsp salt
2 large eggs	3 peaches, sliced
1 tsp vanilla extract	2 tbsp sugar
1 c all-purpose flour	1 tbsp all-purpose flour
1 tsp baking powder	1/4 c apricot jam
2 tbsp brewed dark roast coffee	

1. Preheat oven 350°F.
2. In a large bowl beat butter and sugar with mixer on medium speed for 30 seconds.
3. Add eggs and vanilla; beat until thoroughly combined.
4. Stir in 1 cup flour, baking powder, cinnamon and salt. Set aside.
5. Combine sugar and 1 tablespoon flour. Sprinkle over peach slices; toss to coat.
6. Fold peaches into batter. Pour into 9x9x2 inch cake pan.
7. Bake until wooden pick inserted near the center comes out clean, 50 to 55 minutes.
8. Set aside in pan to cool.
9. In a small saucepan, combine jam and coffee.
10. Bring to a boil. Spread evenly over cake.
11. Serve warm or at room temperature.

Apple Cinnamon Walnut Coffee Cake

2 c all-purpose flour

1 c granulated sugar

1/2 c sour cream

1/2 softened butter

1/4 cup milk

1/4 c brewed medium roast coffee

2 medium (2 c) peeled and chopped apples

2 large eggs

1 tsp baking powder

1 tsp baking soda

1 tsp vanilla extract

1/4 tsp salt

Topping:

1/2 c chopped walnuts or pecans

1/2 c firmly brown sugar

1 tbsp melted butter

1 tsp ground cinnamon

1. Preheat oven to 350 ºF.
2. Combine all cake ingredients except apples in large mixing bowl.
3. Beat at medium speed, scraping bowl often, until smooth (2 to 3 minutes).
4. Gently fold in apples by hand.
5. Spread batter into greased 13 x 9-inch baking pan.
6. Combine all topping ingredients in small bowl.
7. Sprinkle over batter.
8. Bake for 30 to 35 minutes or until toothpick inserted in center comes out clean.

Kahlua Banana Coffee Cake

1 c butter, softened   1 tbsp baking powder

1 1/2 c granulated sugar   1 tsp baking soda

1/2 c Kahlua   1 tsp salt

4 large eggs   3/4 c flaked coconut

1/4 c whole milk   3/4 cup chopped walnuts

3 1/2 c sifted all-purpose flour

1 c mashed ripe bananas (2 medium)

1   Preheat oven to 350 °F.
2   Grease and flour 9x9x2 cake pan.
3   Combine butter and sugar, mix until fluffy. Fold in
    flour, 1/2 cup at a time. Add remaining ingredients
    except coconut and nuts.
4   Mix on low speed until mixture is well blended.
    Increase to medium speed, mix 2 more minutes.
5   Stir in coconut and nuts. Turn into prepared pan.
6   Bake 45 to 50 minutes or until golden brown.
    Remove from oven; let stand 10 minutes.
7   Turn onto serving tray

Optional Topping:

1 tbsp dark roasted brewed coffee, cooled
1 c brown sugar

Mix Kahlua and brown sugar, dust over cake.

Chocolate Coffee Cake

1/2 c butter

1 c raw sugar

3 eggs

1 1/2 tbsp vanilla extract

1/4 tsp almond extract

2 c bakers flour

4 oz semisweet chocolate chips

3/4 c brewed coffee (recommend 100% medium roast Kona coffee)

1/2 tsp salt

2 tsp cinnamon

1 tsp baking powder 1/4 tsp baking soda

1/4 c buttermilk

1. Preheat oven to 350 ºF.
2. Grease and flour 2 eight-inch round cake pans Blend in sugar, and eggs until smooth and creamy Mix dry ingredients in separate bowl.
3. Add buttermilk and butter mixture.
4. Combine coffee and chocolate in small saucepan.
5. Heat on low heat until chocolate is melted and mixed with coffee. Add to batter mixture and blend thoroughly.
6. Pour into cake pans, bake about 45 minutes or until firm Ice with Mocha Icing.

Mocha Icing:

1 tsp vanilla extract

1/2 c brewed medium roast coffee

6 oz semisweet chocolate chips

1/4 cup soft butter

Place chocolate, coffee, and vanilla in small saucepan. Heat on low until chocolate is melted and mixed. Remove from heat, blend in butter. Mix well.

Streusel Coffee Cake

1 1/2 c all-purpose flour

3/4 c sugar

2 tsp baking powder

1/4 tsp salt

4 tbsp brewed dark roast coffee

3/4 c semi-sweet chocolate morsels

1 egg, beaten

1/2 c whole milk

1/4 cup cooking oil

1. Preheat oven to 375 °F. Grease and flour 9x9x2 inch cake pan.
2. Combine flour, sugar, baking powder, and salt, mix well.
3. In separate bowl, combine egg, milk, cooking oil and coffee Fold into flour mixture, mix well, and add chocolate morsels.

Topping:

2 tbsp brown sugar

1 tbsp all-purpose flour

1 tsp ground cinnamon

1 tbsp soft butter

Combine dry ingredients, fold in butter until soft and crumbly Sprinkle over cake batter Bake 30 minutes or until golden brown

Sour Cream Coffee Cake

1 c sour cream

2 eggs

1 c sugar

1 1/2 c all-purpose flour

2 tsp baking powder

1/2 tsp baking soda

1/4 tsp salt

2 tbsp brewed dark roast coffee

Crumb Topping:

1/2 cup all-purpose flour

1/4 cup brown sugar

1/4 cup sugar

3 tbsp soft butter

Preheat oven to 350 °F.
Grease and flour 9-inch round cake pan.

Topping:

Blend topping ingredients, blend until mixed and crumbly. Make topping first, and set aside

To make cake:

1. Place eggs in bowl, whip until frothy.
2. Add sour cream, mix until smooth and creamy
    Thoroughly mix in sugar.
3. Add flour, baking powder, baking soda, and salt and
    blend well.
4. Pour into cake pan, sprinkle topping evenly over top
    of batter.
5. Bake 18-20 minutes, or until springy and golden
    brown.

6. Flip onto cooling rack, cool 30 minutes before
   serving.

Note* This recipe make a very light and tender cake
that will not cut smoothly when hot.

INDEX OF RECIPES

Coffee Smoothie 21

Banana Blender 22

Koffe Frappe 22

Caribbean Chiller 23

Espresso Cooler 23

Continental Cooler 24

Tropicana Coffee 24

Icy Mocha Mint 25

Mocha Frosty 25

Cafe Mazagran 25

Coffee Float 26

Cafe Au Vin 26

Homemade Coffee
Smoothie Recipe: 27

Cafe Frappe Recipe 27

Cinnamon Caramel Iced
Coffee 28

Thai Iced Coffee 28

Ginger Fruit Mocha 29

Coffee Frosty 29

Coffee Banana Smoothie
30

Maple Walnut Mocha 31

Banana Frosty 31

Mocha Mist 31

Toffee Coffee 32

LUSH LATTES 33

Tropical Iced Latte 34

Mandarin Chocolate
Latte 34

Cactus Latte 35

Cabo Mocha Latte 35

Mai Tai Latte 35

Raspberry Guava Latte 35

Melba Latte 36

Eggnog Latte 36

Grande Caffe Latte 36

Baklava Latte 37

Mint Mocha Latte 37

Elegantissimo 38

Caramel Nut Latte 38

Blanco Cappuccino 39

ALCOHOLIC COFFEE

DRINKS 41

Café Brulot 42

Frosty Brandy 42

Bandito Coffee 43

Jamaican Kicker 43

Hot Mint Julep 44

Grasshopper 44

Hot Toddy 45

Pina Coffeelada 45

Velvet Hammer 46

Café Vermouth 46

Coffee Liquor 47

Calypso Coffee 47

Irish 48

French Royale 48

Coffee Liqueur 49

Café Vienna 50

Café Bavaria 50

Caribbean Java 51

Cozy Coffee Amaretto 51

Caribbean Cruise 52

Cabo Breeze 52

Café Pari' 53

Irish Warmer 53

El Diablo 54

Espresso Nudge 54

Fruity Rum Heater 55

Cabo Breeze 55

Louisiana Cooler 56

White Russian 56

Café Cognac Cooler 57

Café Vermouth 57

DELECTABLE COFFEE

DESSERTS 59

Tiramisu 60

Kahlua Muffins 61

Beignets 62

Espresso Chocolate Mousse 63

Tarratoga Torte 64

Coffee Toffee Pie 65

Layered Coffee Mousse 66

Cafe Au Lait Pudding 67

Espresso Cheesecake 68

Coffee Chiffon Pie 69

Glazed Coffee Loaf 70

Kealakekua Macadamia Cookies 71

Chocolate Coffee Truffles 72

Coffee Crème Custards 73

Petits Pots de Cappuccino 74

Coffee Zabaglione 75

Sour Cherry Coffee Loaf 76

Orange Coffee Scones 77

Coffee Date Cake 78

Coffee Liqueur Cookies 79

Chocolate Mousse Cake 80

SCRUMPTIOUS COFFEE CAKES 83

Chocolate Mousse Coffee Cake 84

Cinnamon Coffee Cake 85

Coconut Coffee Cake 86

Blueberry Coffee Cake 88

Peach Coffee Cake 89

Apple Cinnamon Walnut Coffee Cake 90

Kahlua Banana Coffee Cake 91

Chocolate Coffee Cake 92

Streusel Coffee Cake 93

Sour Cream Coffee Cake 94